Family Rhymes for Jewish Times

Children's Poems for Shabbat, Holidays and Everyday

by:
Shoshana Silberman
illustrated by:
Karen Ostrove

Published by

THE UNITED SYNAGOGUE OF CONSERVATIVE JUDAISM
COMMISSION ON JEWISH EDUCATION

DEDICATION

"Each child carries his or her own blessing into the world." (Yiddish Proverb)

This book is lovingly dedicated to my grandchildren – Noam Reuven, Jonah Raphael, Yaakov Yehudah, Adira Chana, Meir Simcha, and Chana D'vora – each a great blessing and joy.

S.S.

These poems are meant to be playful and celebratory, reflecting children's experiences of Jewish life. Though primarily geared to the nursery set (ages 3-5), there are numbers of poems in this collection that children in primary grades (ages 5-8) will enjoy, especially when they can read them on their own.

TABLE OF CONTENTS

<u>H</u> and <u>h</u> = the sound of ch as in the composer "Bach"

You will find a glossary at the end of the book which tells a bit about the meaning of the Hebrew terms used in these rhymes for Jewish times.

SHABBAT

TZEDAKAH

Before we light the candles tall,
I dig into my pockets all.
Whatever coins are there, you see,
I'll give to those with less than me.
That's tzedakah, my parents say.
We need to give before we pray.

Can I?

Mom, can I invite a friend,
To share Shabbat from start to end?
Dad, can I help with the meal?
If you agree, I'll make a deal.
I'll pick up toys; sweep with a broom.
I'll make my bed and clean my room!

Shabbat Shalom

Candles, <u>h</u>allah, flowers and wine,
My Shabbat table looks so fine!
Soup and salad, chicken galore,
Will I have room for any more?
So many yummy foods to take:
Noodle kugel and choc'late cake.

SHARING SHABBAT

I love grape juice, so please don't stop.
Fill my kiddush cup to the top.
From that <u>h</u>allah, I'll have a slice.
I think Shabbat is really nice.

It's not just dinner, which is good.
We're all together, like we should.
We stop and listen with delight
And share Shabbat — now that feels right.

B'YAHAD
(Together)

My dad burned the kugel.
My mom spilled the wine.
The dog ate the chicken.
She barked to say, "It's fine!"

The meal is really great!
I like it a whole lot.
'Cause we all eat together,
I love it on Shabbat.

Havdalah Question

Is it in a garden or a creek?
Where is Shabbat during the week?
Say Havdalah, sing songs and then,
When will Shabbat come back again?
With wine and candle, spices, too,
Let's say goodbye, shalom, to you.
We'll give Shabbat a little rest
Though it's the time we love the best.

ROSH HASHANAH

DIP, DROP

Dipping apples into honey,
Such a mess, it isn't funny.
"It's Rosh Hashanah," says my Dad.
"I'll show you how, you'll be so glad.
"Keep your apple on the table,
"Move in closer. Yes, you're able.
"Hold it right above your dish;
"Dip it in, and make a wish.
"Have a year that's very sweet.
"Now, quickly eat your apple treat!"

THE SHOFAR

I huffed and puffed and blew it,
But not a sound came out.
I don't know how to do it.
I guess I'll have to shout:
    "Tekiah!"
    "Teruah!"
    "Sh'varim!"
    "Tekiah G'dolah!"

TURN AND LEARN

Teshuvah: turn,
We'll change our ways.
Torah: learn,
All of our days.

YOM KIPPUR

FASTING

No, not an apple or a pear,
Not even grapes for them to share.
My parents fast; they don't eat food.
They say it helps to set the mood,
To think, to pray throughout the day.
"I'm sorry, God," I hear them say.

TOO YOUNG

You're much too young, too young to fast.
For one whole day, you'd never last.
And so, for now, give up a treat,
One thing you really like to eat.
Now, think of growing big and strong,
And learning what is right and wrong.
For as you learn to be a Jew,
Just know that we are proud of you.

SUKKOT

TOGETHER

The lulav is king;
He stands straight and tall.
The etrog is queen;
Do not let her fall!
Together, shake them all around.
In every place, God can be found.

FULL OF PRIDE

Through the branches, I see stars,
Jupiter and even Mars.
In here, I am so full of pride;
I never want to go outside.
In this sukkah that I helped build,
Just sitting here, I am so thrilled.

THANK GOD

Fruits and gourds and special light
Shimmer in the crisp, fall night.
Cards and pictures all around,
Leaves that make a crunching sound.
Hang that apple; hang that lime;
Sukkot is a special time.
Thank God for this holy space.
Thank God for this special place.

SIMHAT TORAH

CELEBRATE

Look who's coming — Dave and Dan,
Jennifer and little Ann,
Gabe and Sharon, Sarah, too,
Adam, Jon, Ronit and Sue.
All are here to celebrate
Simhat Torah – Wow! It's great!

11

HURRY UP

Seven chances to march around,
We're dancing with a joyous sound.
We're waving flags high in the air,
I never once sit on my chair.
I will not stop until the end,
While wishing we could march again.

TORAH JOY

When we open the ark we sing.
Dance with the Torah in a ring.
I have my little Torah, too.
Come join us, and we'll dance with you!

HANUKKAH

Too Much?

Eight days long is too much time
For candles standing in a line,
For gifts and latkes, dreidles, too,
For friends who visit me and you.
"I think it's too much fun," I say,
"Can't Hanukkah be just one day?
"I'm only kidding; have you guessed?
"I like Hanukkah the best!"

Todah Rabbah
(Thank You Very Much)

Made my mom a paper flower;
Gave my dad soap for his shower.
Bought my sister a silver star,
For my brother, a racing car.
With hugs and smiles, they said, "Todah!"
"Thank you so much; Todah Rabbah."

RECIPE

Rush to the nearest grocery store,
I need to make latkes, twenty more!
Buy more potatoes, eggs and flour.
Get oil and cream — the kind that's sour.
The applesauce is for my dad.
If he doesn't have it, he'll be sad.
Peel the potatoes, grate and fry.
Adding onions can make you cry.
Then fry them up, all crisp and brown.
These latkes are the best in town!

JUDAH MACCABEE

Judah was brave, a warrior, too.
Judah was proud to be a Jew.
He told Antiochus, "It will not do,
"For all the Jews to live like you.
"We have the Torah, with its ways.
"We have Shabbat and holidays.
"Give us freedom to work and play,
"To sing and dance and also pray."
I'm glad that Judah made us free.
He was Judah, the Maccabee!

DREIDLE PLEASE

Don't stop at shin.
I'll have to put one in.
Nun's not the one.
'Cause "nothing" isn't fun.
Heh is a lot.
You will get half the pot.
But, gimmel is the best.
You get to keep the rest!

TU BI'SHVAT

WHAT CAN IT BE?

It's paper for notes
And wood for boats.
It's fruit to eat;
Rest from the heat.
It's cool, cool shade
Where dreams are made.
What can it be?
Of course, a tree!

NAMES HELP

Jonathan, Jenny, Shira, too,
Just what can each one of you do
To end pollution in our time?
Recycle. Renew. It's cleanup time!

THANK YOU

A sapling on a little hill,
A bean sprout on my window sill —
It's growing up; it's growing out,
So lovely that I want to shout:
"Thank you, God, for planet Earth —
"My happy home since my birth."

HAPPY BIRTHDAY, TREES

The earth has beauty I can see,
Each time I spy a blossom tree.
It's Tu bi'Shvat, so we all say,
To all the trees, "Happy Birthday!"

PURIM

YES, BUT

"If just another sound you make,
"I know my head will surely break."
"But, Dad, it's Purim. Let's all shout.
"For Haman's name, we must drown out!"

"Yes, but can you wait until when
"The story's read in shul again?
"From our house we've not departed.
"The Megillah hasn't started!"

FAMILY FUN

My brother was Haman;
My sister was Esther.
My dad was Mordecai;
And I, the court jester.

Our family
Just looked the best.
We won first prize.
You may have guessed.
Who shall we be
For Purim next year?
Before you know it,
It will be here.

ESTHER

Take a deep breath and try to be brave.
For, Esther, your people you must save.
Tell King Ahasheurus of Haman's plan,
To hurt each Jewish woman and man.
Let the king know we want to be free
And live Jewish lives most happily.
Courage, Esther, here's what you must do:
Help save the life of every Jew!

THE BEST HAMANTASH

"This is the best hamantash I've had,
"Just biting into it makes me glad.
"Delicious dough with cherries inside,
"Way down to my stomach, it does slide.
"It is the best I've eaten," I say.
"'Cause it's my first hamantash today."

18

PESA<u>H</u>

THEY'RE HERE!

Packed in a carton, ever so tight,
Up from the basement, into the light.
The Pesa<u>h</u> dishes are here to stay
For all eight days of the holiday.

MY JOB

My job is <u>h</u>aroset — chop, chop
From sunup to sunset — chop, chop.
Add some apples and wine — chop, chop
This <u>h</u>aroset is mine — chop, chop.

WE'RE READY

The house is so clean; just see it shine.
Boxes of matzah are in a line.
We have eggs and apples, jelly, too.
There's honey and nuts for me and you.
The guests are all here; I know my part.
We are all ready; so, now, let's start!

I Can't Wait

I can't wait for the seder to start.
The Four Questions I know by heart.
I like showing off, once in a while.
It makes my grandpa really smile.
And grandma, too, looks very proud
When I ask those questions out loud.
But, most of all, it pleases me
To know I'm learning steadily.
Before you know it, I'll be grown;
And I'll have children of my own.
They'll want to have the seder start.
The Four Questions they'll know by heart.

It's Funny

In the middle of the seder meal,
The afikomen I try to steal.
But, when the leader "buys" it back,
I hand it over in a sack.
For this, I get a special treat.
This afikomen thing is neat!

QUESTIONS

"If I can't ask the questions four,
"Would you, please, hug me even more?"

"Of course, my dear," my mother sighed,
"There is next year; I know you tried."

"So, maybe I will do just one.
"'Cause that would be a lot of fun!
"Well, maybe two or even three —
"Now, won't that make you proud of me?"

"Yes, I'm proud when you do your best.
"The Four Questions is not a test.
"When you are ready, that's the time.
"Then you can start that famous line...."

*Mah nishtanah halailah hazeh
mikol halelot?*

HELP

Cloths are dusting, mops are mopping.
Mixers whirling, blades are chopping.
I'd better tell them. Yes, I must.
"Don't get me mixed in with the dust!
"Please do your cleaning carefully.
"I'm not <u>h</u>ametz; don't sweep up ME!"

YOM HA'ATZMA'UT

YOM HULEDET
(Happy Birthday)

We had a birthday party
With some cake and ice cream, too.
We all sang Yom Huledet
To a flag that's white and blue.

It's Israel's Happy Birthday,
A day of jubilation.
It's Israel's Happy Birthday,
A day of celebration.

ISRAEL

Long ago our people
Walked on this golden sand.
And long ago the Jews
Lived in the Promised Land.
Today, Israelis say,
"*Shalom*," to every Jew.
"Won't you come to Israel?
"We surely hope you do!"

A WISH

For Israel, on her birthday,
I will plant a tiny tree.
Yehi Haydad, Hip Hurray,
It's a gift to her from me.

So with my friend from Israel,
We make the country bloom.
And with my friend from Israel,
I'd like to visit soon.

22

TEN GOOD RULES

I am God, there is no other.
Honor your father and your mother.
With great respect, you will say God's name.
(For when you say it, it's not a game.)
Remember Shabbat, our holy day —
A day to rest, to rejoice and pray.
Do not murder; don't you lie, or take
What isn't your own, for heaven's sake!
These rules are a gift from God to you.
They'll help you be a very good Jew.

TORAH TALK

We left Egypt very free —
No responsibility.
Then, the Torah came our way
To help us live, day-by-day.
From the Torah we can learn:
Show respect and show concern.

EVERY DAY

BOKER TOV
(Good Morning)

Boker Tov, I'm ready to go.
I want to play in all the snow
That fell so softly through the night
And glimmered in the morning light.

Before I go, I want to say,
"Thank You, God, for another day.
"Keep me safe whenever I play.
"Please, let me have a happy day."

LAILAH TOV
(Good Night)

Shhhh! Quiet! It's time for bed,
But I won't sleep till Sh'ma is said.
Every night, when day is done,
I whisper to the Holy One.
Every night, when day is done,
I tell the world that God is one.

NEW SISTER

Listen to me, my little one.
We have good news to tell you, son.
Tomorrow will be a special day
A baby sister's on her way.

"But, I was hoping for a bike.
"It is what I would really like.
"Do we need a brand new baby?
"Sure, I guess I'll like her — maybe."

She will be cute and very sweet.
Maybe you'll think she's quite a treat.
But, you'll still be our number one,
Our very own dear, first-born son.

You'll play and count, 1-2-3-4.
You'll teach her Aleph Bet and more,
Like blessing candles, bread and wine.
Now, don't you think it will be fine?

Okay, okay, oh me, oh my,
I sure hope that she doesn't cry!
But if she does, please have no fears…
I'll stick my fingers in my ears!

SHARE

God made chicken soup and rice,
Pizza pies that taste so nice.
Peanut butter, ice cream, too,
Are good foods for me and you.

We need to say a Thank You prayer,
And then remember we must share.
Do bring food to those in need.
All the hungry, we must feed.

UNCLE GABE

When Uncle Gabe comes here to stay,
Then all we do is play and play.
We like to go to a nearby park,
And swing and slide until it's dark.

When we come back, we take a look
At pictures in a special book.
It is our family treasure,
Giving us a lot of pleasure.

After dinner, it's bath and bed,
And that is when the Sh'ma is said.
He teaches me to be a Jew;
He knows what we're supposed to do.

Do you have a person who
Is this wonderful to you?

TO SAVTA'S HOUSE
(To Grandma's House)

Hurry, scurry like a mouse,
Pack your bags for Savta's house.
Take a toothbrush and a comb,
Warm PJ's and toys from home.
She'll read us stories. It's a treat.
We will get tasty foods to eat.
(Before we take a single bite,
We say a blessing, 'cause that's right.)
We feel so special when we go;
We know we're loved from head to toe.

SABA'S GARDEN
(Grandpa's Garden)

My Saba has a garden
With green beans and tomatoes,
Eggplants, peas and cucumbers —
No Idaho potatoes!

Sunflowers and red roses,
We smell them with our noses.
Herbs for use in cooking, too,
But they make me sneeze, "kerchoo!"

My dear Saba has a way
Of making work seem like play.
I'm a very lucky boy.
I have Saba to enjoy.

BUBBE
(Great-grandmother)

Do you have a bubbe? Well, I do.
My bubbe is almost ninety-two!
She's so very old, as you can see;
And she is so very good to me.
Whenever I dance or sing a song,
Bubbe always claps and sings along.
Her eyes light up. They're full of glee;
Every single time she looks at me.

GLOSSARY OF HEBREW WORDS

This glossary is arranged in the order in which the Hebrew words appear in the book. The **word** in **bold** indicates a title of a new section.

Shabbat = The Sabbath is a day of rest, cessation from work, and a time for prayer, family and joy.

Tzedakah = Charity, comes from the root word tzadek, meaning justice. We have an obligation to act justly toward those in need by providing them with necessities and a sense of dignity.

Kiddush = A prayer intoned over wine, declaring the sanctity of the Shabbat. The gathering after Shabbat morning service is also called "Kiddush" because the prayer over wine is intoned.

Hallah = A loaf of bread, oblong or round in shape, it is often braided. Hallah is used on Sabbath and holidays. On these days there are 2 loaves of hallot (pl.).

Kugel = A traditional baked dish made with mashed potatoes or noodles. It is often served on Shabbat and holidays.

B'Yahad = Together.

Havdalah = A ceremony at the end of the Sabbath (Saturday night) in which the Shabbat is sent away with blessings on wine, the fragrance of spices and the light of a candle.

Shalom = The word for hello and goodbye. It means "peace."

Rosh Hashanah = The Jewish New Year. It comes in the Fall.

Shofar = A musical instrument made from a ram's horn which is sounded during the Rosh Hashanah service and at the end of Yom Kippur.

Tekiah = One of the sounds (blasts) of the shofar.

Teruah = Three shorter blasts of the shofar.

Sh'varim = A staccato blast of the shofar made up of a series of short blasts.

Tekiah G'dolah = A loud crescendo blast of the shofar.

Teshuvah = Repentence. From the Hebrew root word "to return."

Yom Kippur = The holiest day of the Jewish calendar. A 25-hour fast day from sundown to after nightfall the following day, it is a time spent in synagogue prayer, reflection and teshuvah.

Sukkot = The seven-day Festival of Booths when Jews take their festive meals in temporary structures with a roof made of wood or branches opened to the sky. Coming fourteen days after Rosh Hashanah, it celebrates the completion of the harvest of grain and wine in Israel. It commemorates the dwelling of the Israelites in booths in the desert after the Exodus from Egypt. It is followed immediately by Shemini Atzeret and Simhat Torah.

Lulav = The lulav and etrog go together. The lulav consists of a palm branch, three myrtle branches, and two willow branches. A blessing is said over the lulav and etrog during the festival of Sukkot and they are shaken during the recitation of psalms. They are paraded around the synagogue while a prayer is chanted.

Etrog = Is a lemon-like fruit called a "citron." There are many interpretations of the meaning of the lulav and etrog. They are a reminder of our agricultural dependence and the ever-presence of God.

Sukkah = The temporary structure in which Jews take their meals during Sukkot (see above).

Simhat Torah = The holiday for rejoicing in the Torah, it celebrates the end of the yearly Torah reading cycle in the synagogue and its immediate resumption with Genesis. The rejoicing is characterized by seven processions with the Torot (plural of Torah) around the synagogue with dancing and singing.

Torah = The Pentateuch, the Five Books of Moses. In the synagogue, there are Torah scrolls. The Torah scroll is read in Hebrew on Shabbat and holidays.

Hanukkah = The Festival of Lights is an eight-day celebration of the victory of the Maccabees over the Assyrian-Greek regime which sought to impose restrictions in Israel against Jewish practices and values. In 165 B.C.E. the Temple in Jerusalem was recaptured and purified and political sovereignty was restored.

Todah Rabbah = "Thank you very much" in Hebrew.

Judah Maccabee = The leader of the Israelite rebellion, seeking freedom from the Assyrian Greeks.

Antiochus = The ruler of the Assyrian-Greek empire.

Dreidle = A spinning top with Hebrew letters that begin the Hebrew words meaning "Great Miracle Happened There." During Hanukkah Jews play a game of put-and-take with the dreidle.

Shin   }
Nun   } = Hebrew letters that begin the Hebrew words for a "Great Miracle Happened
Heh   }   There."
Gimmel}

Tu Bi'shvat = Jewish arbor day known as the New Year of the Trees which comes during the winter in North America but at the beginning of spring in Israel. Trees are planted by school children in Israel and we eat fruits, particularly fruits from the Land of Israel.

Purim = A day of joy marked by the reading of the biblical Scroll of Esther, the exchange of food gifts, and the giving of tzedakah (charity) to the poor. On Purim we read the Megillah (scroll) which tells the story of the courage of Esther and the deliverance of the Jews from the hands of Haman who endeavored to wipe them out.

Haman = The viceroy of Persia, who attempted to exterminate the Jews.

Shul = Synagogue.

Megillah = The scroll from which the story of the saving of the Jews from the hands of wicked Haman by Mordecai and Esther is read.

Esther = A Jewish heroine in the story of Purim. Esther becomes Queen of Persia and at the urging of her uncle, Mordecai, intervenes with the King and overturns Haman's plot to exterminate the Jews.

Mordecai = The uncle of Esther (see above).

Hamantash = A three-cornered pastry with filling. It is eaten on Purim and supposedly resembles Haman's hat or pockets.

Pesaḥ = Passover is the spring festival marking the liberation from slavery of the Israelites from Egypt. Its basic focus is the seder, a home celebration, at which the saga of the Exodus is retold.

Ḥaroset = One of several special foods eaten as part of the ritual of the Passover meal, it is a mixture of nuts, apples, raisins, and wine and reminds us of the bricks the Israelite slaves were forced to make.

Four Questions = These questions are asked by the children at the Passover meal They ask about changes in the meal which are particular to Passover and serve as a stimulus for the telling of the Exodus tale.

Mah nishtanah halailah hazeh mikol halelot? = "Why is this night different from all other nights?" is the opening line of the Four Questions, part of the Passover seder.

Ḥametz = Leaven and foods containing leaven, which is proscribed during the eight days of Passover.

Seder = The order of the Passover meal and attendant readings. The Passover meal with its rituals and readings is called the "seder."

Afikomen = A matzah which is set aside during the seder and is eaten after the meal is concluded.

Yom Ha'atzma'ut = Israel Independence Day.

Yom Huledet = Birthday.

"Shalom" = Hello or goodbye; it means peace.

Yehi Haydad = Yay! Hurrah!

Shavu'ot = A late spring holiday, seven weeks after Passover. Partially an agricultural festival celebrating the grain harvest in Israel and the bringing of the first fruits, it celebrates the revelation at Sinai and the giving of the Torah.

Every Day

Boker Tov = Good morning.

Lailah Tov = Good night.

Sh'ma = A biblical passage which is recited twice a day (morning and evening) as a declaration of faith. It also is recited before going to sleep.

Aleph Bet = First two Hebrew letters. Hebrew for "alphabet."

Savta's = Grandma's (in Hebrew).

Saba's = Grandpa's (in Hebrew).

Bubbe = Grandmother or great-grandmother (in Yiddish).